Teach Yourself Great Web Design in a Week

Anne-Rae Vasquez-Peterson

Paul Chow

Sams.net Publishing
201 W. 103rd Street
Indianapolis, IN 46290

Teach Yourself Great Web Design in a Week

Publisher and President:	Richard K. Swadley
Publishing Manager:	Mark Taber
Acquisitions Manager	Beverly M. Eppink
Director of Editorial Services:	Cindy Morrow
Assistant Marketing Managers:	Kristina Perry
	Rachel Wolfe